China's Military Modernization and Cyber Activities

Testimony of Dr. Larry M. Wortzel before the House Armed Services Committee

As a member of the US-China Economic and Security Review Commission, I will present some of the commission's findings on China's military modernization, US-China security relations, and China's cyber activities from the *2013 Annual Report to Congress*.[1] The views I present today, however, are my own. I want to acknowledge the fine work of our staff in preparing the annual report and especially the excellent research of our foreign policy and security staff in helping to prepare this testimony.

China's Military Modernization

China's military, the People's Liberation Army (PLA), is undergoing an extensive modernization program that presents significant challenges to US security interests in Asia. This modernization includes creating a surveillance and strike architecture that supports operations at longer distances away from China's coast. It makes the PLA a more formidable force in all the dimensions of war: air, space, land, sea, and in the electromagnetic spectrum. The PLA has new, multimission-capable combat ships, aircraft, submarines, and new generations of missiles.

First and foremost, major elements of this program—such as the DF-21D antiship ballistic missile and increasing numbers of advanced submarines armed with antiship cruise missiles—are designed to restrict US freedom of action throughout the Western Pacific. The PLA is rapidly expanding and diversifying its ability to conduct conventional strikes against US and allied bases, ships, and aircraft throughout the region, including those that it previously could not reach with conventional weapons, such as US military facilities on Guam. As the PLA's anti-access/area-denial capabilities mature, the costs and risks to the United States for intervention in a potential regional conflict involving China will increase.[2] The Chinese military, of course, sensitive to nineteenth and twentieth century history, thinks of these actions as counterintervention strategies designed to prevent foreign militaries from intervening in China's sovereign affairs or territory.

Furthermore, the PLA's rapidly advancing regional power projection capabilities enhance Beijing's ability to use force against Taiwan, Japan, and rival claimants in the South China Sea. More seriously, because China's military doctrine emphasizes preemptive attacks, it raises the stakes in any crisis. Many potential security scenarios could require the US military to defend US regional allies and partners as well as maintain open and secure access to the air and maritime commons in the Western Pacific.

At the same time, rising unease over both China's expanding capabilities and increasing assertiveness is driving US allies and partners in Asia to improve their own military forces and strengthen their security relationships with each other. These trends could support US interests in Asia by lightening Washington's operational responsibilities in the region. On the other hand, if China's neighbors pursue military capabilities that could be used offensively or preemptively due to the perception that the United States will be unable to follow through on its commitment to the rebalance to Asia, this could undermine US interests in the region.

In the commission's 2013 annual report we discuss the following main developments in China's military modernization:

Navy

Aircraft Carriers. Since commissioning its first aircraft carrier, the *Liaoning*, in September 2012, China continues to develop a fixed-wing carrier aviation capability, which is necessary for the carrier to carry out air defense and offensive strike missions. The *Liaoning* is a former Russian aircraft carrier purchased from the Ukraine. It was refitted and modernized in China. The PLA Navy conducted its first successful carrier-based takeoff and landing with the Jian-15 (J-15) in November 2012, certified its first group of aircraft carrier pilots and landing signal officers on the carrier's first operational deployment from June to July 2013, and verified the flight deck operations process in September 2013.[3] The *Liaoning* will continue to conduct short deployments and shipboard aviation training until 2015 to 2016, when China's first J-15 regiment is expected to become operational. The J-15 is a Chinese copy of the Russian Su-33. China likely intends to follow the *Liaoning* with at least two domestically produced hulls. The first of these appears to be under construction and could become operational before 2020.

Submarine-Launched Ballistic Missiles. China's Julang-2 (JL-2) submarine-launched ballistic missile is expected to reach initial operational capability very soon.[4] The missile has been under development for a number of years, which shows that Chinese military industries still have some problems in developing and fielding new systems. The JL-2, when mated with the PLA Navy's Jin-class nuclear ballistic missile submarine (SSBN), will give China its first credible sea-based nuclear deterrent. The Jin SSBN/JL-2 weapon system will have a range of approximately 4,000 nautical miles, allowing the PLA Navy to target the continental United States from China's littoral waters.[5] China has deployed three Jin SSBNs and probably will field two additional units by 2020.[6]

Sea-Based Land Attack Capability. China currently does not have the ability to strike land targets with sea-based cruise missiles. However, the PLA Navy is developing a land attack capability, likely for its Type-095 guided-missile attack submarine and Luyang III guided-missile destroyer. Modern submarines and surface combatants armed with land attack cruise missiles (LACM) will complement the PLA's growing inventory of air- and ground-based LACMs and ballistic missiles, enhancing Beijing's flexibility for attacking land targets throughout the Western Pacific, including US facilities in Guam.[7]

Shipbuilding. The PLA Navy continues to steadily increase its inventory of modern submarines and surface combatants. China is known to be building seven classes of ships simultaneously but may be constructing additional classes.[8] Trends in China's defense spending, research and development, and shipbuilding suggest the PLA Navy will continue to modernize. By 2020, China could have approximately 60 submarines that are able to employ submarine-launched intercontinental ballistic missiles, torpedoes, mines, or antiship cruise missiles. China's surface combat force also has modernized and expanded with approximately 75 surface combatants that are able to conduct multiple missions or that have been extensively upgraded since 1992.[9] The combat fleets are supported by a combat logistics force that can conduct underway replenishment and limited repairs. All of these ships will be equipped to take advantage of a networked, redundant command, control, communications, computer, intelligence, surveillance, and reconnaissance system (C4ISR) fielded by the PLA.

Attack Submarines. China has a formidable force of 63 diesel-electric and nuclear attack submarines.[10] They are equipped with nuclear and conventional torpedoes and mines as well as antiship cruise missiles.[11] In 2012, China began building four "improved variants" of its *Shang*-class nuclear attack submarine. China also continues production of the *Yuan*-class diesel-electric submarine—some of which will include an air-independent propulsion system that allows for extended duration operations—and the *Jin*-class SSBN. Furthermore, China is developing two new classes of nuclear submarines and may jointly design and build four advanced diesel-electric submarines with Russia.[12] China's growing submarine inventory will significantly enhance China's ability to strike opposing surface ships throughout the Western Pacific and to protect future nuclear deterrent patrols and aircraft carrier task groups.[13]

Air Force

Fighter Aircraft. China also is developing two next-generation fighters, the J-20 and the J-31, which could feature low observability and active electronically scanned array radar.[14] The PLA Air Force conducted the first test flights of the J-20 and J-31 in January 2011 and October 2012, respectively.[15] These aircraft will strengthen China's ability to project power and gain and maintain air superiority in a regional conflict.

Cargo Transport Aircraft. In January 2013, China conducted the first test flight of its indigenously developed cargo transport aircraft, the Yun-20 (Y-20). China previously was unable to build heavy transport aircraft, so it has relied on a small number of Russian Ilyushin-76 (IL-76) aircraft for strategic airlift since the 1990s. Aircraft specifications provided by official Chinese media indicate the Y-20 can carry about twice the cargo load of the IL-76 and about three times the cargo load of the US C-130.[16] The Y-20 will enhance the PLA's ability to respond to internal security crises and border contingencies, support military international peacekeeping and humanitarian assistance operations, and project power in a regional conflict.[17] The larger aircraft and expanded fleet will enhance the PLA's capability to employ the 15th Airborne Army, part of the PLA Air Force.

LACM-Capable Bomber Aircraft. In June 2013, the PLA Air Force began to receive new Hongzha-6K (H-6K) bomber aircraft. The H-6K, an improved variant of the H-6 (originally adapted from a late-1950s Soviet design), has extended range of around 2,400 to 3,100 miles and can carry China's new long-range LACM, the CJ-10. The CJ-10 has a range of around 900 to 1,200 miles.[18] The bomber/LACM weapon system provides the PLA Air Force with the ability to conduct conventional strikes against regional targets throughout the Western Pacific, including US facilities in Guam.[19] Although the H-6K airframe could be modified to carry a nuclear-tipped air-launched LACM, and China's LACMs likely have the ability to carry a nuclear warhead, there is no evidence to confirm China is deploying nuclear warheads on any of its air-launched LACMs.[20] The H-6K also may be able to carry supersonic antiship cruise missiles.[21]

Space and Counterspace

In May 2013, China fired a rocket into nearly geosynchronous Earth orbit, marking the highest known suborbital launch since the US Gravity Probe A in 1976 and China's highest known suborbital launch to date. Although Beijing claims the launch was part of a high-altitude scientific experiment, available data suggest China was testing the launch vehicle component of a new high-altitude antisatellite (ASAT) capability.[22] If true, such a test would signal China's intent to develop an ASAT capability to target satellites in an altitude range that includes the US global positioning system (GPS) and many US military and intelligence satellites. In a potential conflict, this capability could allow China to threaten the US military's ability to detect foreign missiles and provide secure communications, navigation, and precision missile guidance.

Furthermore, in September 2013, China launched a satellite into space from the Jiuquan Satellite Launch Center in western China. Our annual report cites commentary from Gregory Kulacki of the Union of Concerned Scientists, who believes that this launch may represent a capacity to launch new satellites in the event China suffers losses in space from space combat.[23]

China also has improved its ballistic missile defense capabilities by fielding the Russian-made SA-20B surface-to-air missile (SAM) system. In some cases, China's domestically produced CSA-9 SAM system should also be capable of intercepting ballistic missiles.[24]

On 27 December 2012, China announced its Beidou regional satellite navigation system is fully operational and available for commercial use. Using 16 satellites and a network of ground stations, Beidou provides subscribers in Asia with 24-hour precision navigation and timing services.[25] China plans to expand Beidou into a global satellite navigation system by 2020.[26] Beidou is a critical part of China's stated goal to prepare for fighting wars under "informationized conditions," which includes a heavy emphasis on developing the PLA's C4ISR and electronic warfare capabilities. The PLA is integrating Beidou into its systems to improve its command and control and long-range precision strike capabilities and reduce the PLA's reliance on foreign precision navigation and timing services such as GPS.[27]

Strategic Intercontinental Ballistic Missiles

China is enhancing its nuclear deterrent capability by modernizing its nuclear force. It is taking measures such as developing a new road-mobile intercontinental ballistic missile (ICBM), the DF-41. This missile could be equipped with a multiple independently targetable reentry vehicle (MIRV), allowing it to carry as many as 10 nuclear warheads.[28] In addition to MIRVs, China could also equip its ballistic missiles with penetration aids and may be developing the capability to transport ICBMs by train.[29] Furthermore, according to the DoD's 2011 report to Congress on China's military, the PLA "has developed and utilized [underground facilities] since deploying its oldest liquid-fueled missile systems and continues to utilize them to protect and conceal their newest and most modern solid-fueled mobile missiles."[30]

Defense Spending

To support its military modernization, China continued to increase defense spending in 2013. In March, China announced its official defense budget for 2013 rose 10.7 percent in nominal terms to $117.39 billion, signaling the new leadership's support for the PLA's ongoing modernization efforts. This figure represents 5.3 percent of total government outlays and approximately 1.3 percent of estimated gross domestic product (GDP).[31] China's official annual defense budget now has increased for 22 consecutive years and more than doubled since 2006. Most Western analysts agree Beijing likely will retain the ability—even with slower growth rates of its GDP and government revenue—to fund its ongoing military modernization.[32]

It is difficult to estimate China's actual defense spending due to the uncertainty involved in determining how China's purchasing power parity affects the cost of China's foreign military purchases and domestic goods and services, as well as Beijing's omission of major defense-related expenditures. Some purchases of advanced weapons, research and development programs, domestic security spending, and local government support to the PLA are not included in China's official figures on defense spending. The Institute of International Strategic Studies assesses China's actual defense spending is 40 to 50 percent higher than the official figure.[33] The US Department of Defense estimated China's actual defense spending in 2012 fell between $135 and $215 billion, or approximately 20 to 90 percent higher than its announced defense budget.[34]

US-China Security Relations

US-China military-to-military relations deepened and expanded in 2013 after several years of setbacks. From 2012 to 2013, the number of US-China military-to-military contacts more than doubled from approximately 20 to 40.[35] In particular, contact between the US Navy and the PLA Navy increased significantly during this time frame. Key military-to-military contacts in 2013 included the first port visit by a US Navy ship to China since 2009, the first port visit by a Chinese ship to the United States since 2006, and the second ever US-China counterpiracy exercise. Additionally, China in March 2013 accepted the invitation, first extended by then Secretary of Defense Leon Panetta in September 2012, to participate in the US-led multilateral Rim of the Pacific Exercise near Hawaii in 2014.[36]

The DoD contends that a strong military-to-military relationship develops familiarity at the operational level. The department argues that this reduces the risk of conflict through accidents and miscalculations, builds lines of communication at the strategic level that could be important during a crisis, contributes to better overall bilateral relations, and creates opportunities to obtain greater contributions from China to international security. US Pacific Command commander ADM Samuel Locklear in July 2013 said, "The progress that we're making between our two militaries is quite commendable . . . because we are able to have very good dialogue on areas where we converge, and there are a lot of places where we converge as two nations, and we're also able to directly address in a matter-of-fact way where we diverge."[37]

There have been eight rounds of strategic dialogue between China and the United States, currently managed by the Pacific Forum–CSIS. This is a Track 1.5 dialogue that involves some representatives from the US government in attendance, but virtually all Chinese participants are from some part of their government. The past several rounds of the dialogue have dealt with some of the most important strategic issues facing China and the United States, including nuclear strategic stability; the relationship between cyber attacks, space warfare, and nuclear stability; ballistic missile defense; and strategic early warning. Officers from China's strategic missile forces have been in attendance at the dialogue. I see this as one of the most productive dialogues taking place with China. The PLA is an active participant. Ideally such discussions should be direct, government-to-government talks, but it is encouraging that the PLA and the Chinese Foreign Ministry are engaged on these matters.

In another positive development, in mid-November, the US Army and the PLA ground forces conducted their first ever field exercise together. The exercise was focused on disaster relief and took place in Hawaii.[38]

My own experience in direct military-to-military contacts with China leads me to advise caution in what we do with the PLA and what we show them. In my opinion, the wise limitations placed by Congress on military exchanges with China in the National Defense Authorization Act (NDAA) of 2000 should not be lifted. The commission's annual report also reflects this sentiment. Military-to-military contacts with China require careful oversight to ensure that the United States does not improve China's capability against our own forces, Taiwan, or our friends and allies in the Asia-Pacific region.

Enhanced military-to-military contacts between China and the United States in 2013 took place in the context of China's efforts to rebrand the bilateral relationship as a "new type of major-country relationship." This concept, promoted heavily in 2013 by Chinese President Xi Jinping and other high-level Chinese officials, posits the United States and China should, as two major powers, seek to cooperate on a range of bilateral and global issues while avoiding the kind of harmful competition that often characterizes relationships between dominant powers and rising ones.[39] Cooperation is a good thing, but US military leaders cannot lose sight of the PLA's record on human rights. This dictates practical limitations on what we do with China's armed forces. The principal mission of China's military is to keep the Chinese Communist Party (CCP) in power, as we saw in the way that the PLA was used during the 4 June 1989 Tiananmen Massacre and in Tibet.

China's Cyber Activities

While China continues to develop its navy, air force, missile forces, and space and counterspace capabilities, in Chinese military writings, cyberspace is an increasingly important component of China's comprehensive national power and a critical element of its strategic competition with the United States.[40] Beijing seems to recognize that the United States' current advantages in cyberspace are allowing Washington to collect intelligence, exercise command and control of military forces, and support military operations. At the same time, China's leaders fear that the United States may use the open Internet and cyber operations to threaten the CCP's legitimacy.

Since the commission's *2012 Annual Report to Congress*, strong evidence has emerged that the Chinese government is directing and executing a large-scale cyber espionage campaign against the United States. China to date has compromised a range of US networks, including those of DoD and private enterprises. These activities are designed to achieve a number of broad security, political, and economic objectives.

There are no indications the public exposure of Chinese cyber espionage in technical detail throughout 2013 has led China to change its attitude toward the use of cyber espionage to steal intellectual property and proprietary information. The report by Mandiant, a US private cyber-security firm, about the cyber espionage activities of PLA Unit 61398 merely led the unit to make changes to its cyber "tools and infrastructure" to make future intrusions harder to detect and attribute.[41] There are about 16 technical reconnaissance (signals intelligence) units and bureaus in the PLA and at least seven electronic warfare and electronic countermeasures units.[42] Each of China's seven military regions is supported by an electronic countermeasures regiment, and it looks like the PLA Second Artillery Force has its own supporting unit.[43] These organizations focus on cyber penetrations, cyber espionage, and electronic warfare.

When confronted with public accusations from the United States about its cyber espionage, Beijing usually attempts to refute evidence by pointing to the anonymity of cyberspace and the lack of verifiable technical forensic data. It also shifts the media focus by portraying itself as the victim of Washington's cyber activities and calling for greater international cooperation on cyber security.[44] In a press conference on the day after Mandiant released its report in February 2013, a spokesperson for China's Ministry of Foreign Affairs said, "Groundless speculation and accusations regarding hacker attacks, for various purposes, is both unprofessional and irresponsible and it is not helpful for solving the problem." He also emphasized cyber attacks are a serious problem for China.[45]

However, a number of public US government reports, admissions by private companies that they have been the target of cyber espionage, investigations by cyber-security firms, and US press reporting contradict Beijing's long-standing denials. While attribution is difficult and takes great skill, trend analysis is allowing cyber-security professionals to develop a more comprehensive understanding of Chinese cyber actors, tools, tactics, techniques, and procedures.

Threats to US National Security

China's cyber espionage against the US government and defense industrial base poses a major threat to US military operations, the security and well-being of US military personnel, the effectiveness of equipment, and readiness. China apparently uses these intrusions to fill gaps in its own research programs, map future targets, gather intelligence on US strategies and plans, enable future military operations, shorten research and development (R&D) timelines for military technologies, and identify vulnerabilities in US systems and develop countermeasures.[46]

Military doctrine in China also calls for attacks on the critical infrastructure of an opponent's homeland in case of conflict. In July 2013, a threat researcher at Trend Micro, a private Japanese cyber-security firm, claimed he had detected a Chinese cyber intrusion, commencing in December 2012, of a honeypot.[47] He had created the honeypot to resemble the industrial control system of a water plant in the United States. The researcher attributed the intrusion to Unit 61398, based on forensic analysis.[48] If true, this suggests Unit 61398 is collecting intelligence on critical infrastructure in addition to other targets. Such activities are consistent with PLA doctrine, which explains that one function of wartime computer network operations is to "disrupt and damage the networks of [an adversary's] infrastructure facilities, such as power systems, telecommunications systems, and educational systems."[49]

A number of instances of Chinese cyber espionage targeting US national security programs have been identified in recent years. In May 2013, the *Washington Post* described a classified report by the Defense Science Board, which lists more than 24 US weapon system designs the board determined were accessed by cyber intruders. The *Washington Post* reported, "Senior military and industry officials with knowledge of the breaches said the vast majority were part of a widening Chinese campaign of espionage against U.S. defense contractors and government agencies." The list includes the Patriot missile system, Aegis ballistic missile defense system, the F/A-18 fighter, the V-22 Osprey multirole combat aircraft, and the Littoral Combat Ship.[50]

Information gained from intrusions into the networks of US military contractors likely improves China's insight into US weapon systems, enables China's development of countermeasures, and shortens China's research and development timelines for military technologies.[51] In addition, the same intrusions Chinese cyber actors use for espionage also could be used to prepare for offensive cyber operations. Chinese cyber actors could place latent capabilities in US software code or hardware components that might be employed in a potential conflict between the United States and China.

There has been concern in recent years about security risks to the DoD's supply chain. In a meeting in May 2013, commissioners and DoD officials discussed the department's interpretation of US law regarding procurement sources. DoD officials indicated a stricter procurement evaluation standard that includes sourcing concerns could be applied only to items on the United States Munitions List. Items outside this list are judged by a different standard, which some officials believe might preclude concerns about the origin of products. For example, items procured for C4ISR maintenance facilities are not subject to stricter scrutiny. Commissioners raised concerns that this interpretation of the law was limiting the department's ability to address potential risks arising from certain procurement sources. Commissioners urged the DoD to expand the purview of the stricter standard to items beyond the munitions list.

The DoD is currently moving in this direction. Section 806 of the NDAA for Fiscal Year 2011 (Public Law 111-383), is intended to address the problem, but it has yet to be fully implemented. Section 806 authorizes the secretary of defense and the secretaries of the Army, Navy, and Air Force to reject procurement sources for information technology on grounds of protecting supply chain security if they receive a recommendation to do so from the DoD.[52] The department is in the process of implementing Section 806, having conducted tabletop exercises and written the Defense Federal Acquisition Regulation Supplement Rule implementing Section 806. As of May the rule was undergoing interagency coordination.[53] These changes to DoD procurement ultimately may provide officials with the flexibility they need to protect all DoD systems. However, progress has been slow and the problem the commissioners highlighted will remain until the new policy is implemented, potentially posing a threat to national security. Therefore, in the *2013 Annual Report* the commission recommends Congress urge the administration to expedite progress in its implementation of Section 806 of the NDAA for Fiscal Year 2011.

Developments in cloud computing in China may present cyber-security risks for US users and providers of cloud computing services and may also have implications for US national security. Based on the findings of a report by Defense Group Inc. for the commission, the relationship between the Ministry of State Security (MSS) and the Chongqing Special Cloud Computing Zone represents a potential espionage threat to foreign companies that might use cloud computing services provided from the zone or base operations there.[54] In addition, the plan to link 21Vianet's data centers in China and Microsoft's data centers in other countries suggests the Chinese government one day may be able to access data centers outside China through Chinese data centers.[55] With concerns about espionage in mind, in the *2013 Annual Report*, the commission recommends Congress direct the administration to prepare an inventory of existing federal use of cloud computing platforms and services and determine where the data storage and computing services are geographically located. Such inventory should be prepared annually and reported to the appropriate committees of jurisdiction.

Cloud computing also could improve the PLA's C4ISR capabilities. DGI writes that cloud computing "could enable more effective and flexible development and deployment of military equipment, while at the same time improving the survivability of the PLA's information systems by endowing them with greater redundancy (allowing a system's capabilities to survive the disabling or destruction of any individual node)."[56]

Threats to US Industry

China's cyber espionage against US commercial firms poses a significant threat to US business interests and competiveness in key industries. This cyber espionage complements traditional human espionage. Through these efforts, the PLA and China's defense industries are able to leapfrog ahead in technologies and systems and fill in gaps in their own research and development capabilities at a considerable savings in time and money. Gen Keith Alexander, commander of US Cyber Command, assessed the cost to US companies of intellectual property theft is about $250 billion a year, although not all the losses are due to Chinese activity.[57] Chinese entities engaging in cyber and other forms of economic espionage likely conclude that stealing intellectual property and proprietary information is much more cost-effective than investing in lengthy R&D programs.[58] These thefts support national science and technology development plans that are centrally managed and directed by the PRC government.

The Chinese government, primarily through the PLA and the Ministry of State Security, supports these activities by providing state-owned enterprises information and data extracted through cyber espionage to improve their competitive edge, cut R&D timetables, and reduce costs. The strong correlation between compromised US companies and those industries designated by Beijing as "strategic" industries further indicates a degree of state sponsorship, and likely even support, direction, and execution of Chinese economic espionage.[59] Such governmental support for Chinese companies enables them to out-compete US companies, which do not have the advantage of leveraging government intelligence data for commercial gain.[60]

It is difficult to quantify the benefits Chinese firms gain from cyber espionage. We do not know everything about the kinds of information that is targeted and taken, nor do we always know which Chinese actor stole the information. Some thefts may take place that are never detected. In terms of business intelligence, some targets of cyber theft likely include information related to negotiations, investments, and corporate strategies including executive e-mails, long-term business plans, and contracts. In addition to cyber theft, Chinese companies almost certainly are acquiring information through traditional espionage activities, which limits our ability to identify the impact of cyber espionage in particular. Nevertheless, it is clear that China not only is the global leader in using cyber methods to steal intellectual property, but also accounts for the majority of global intellectual property theft.[61] Chinese actors have on several occasions in recent years leveraged cyber activities to gain sensitive or proprietary information from US enterprises:

- In the report by Mandiant mentioned earlier, there is evidence that since 2006 PLA Unit 61398 has penetrated the networks of at least 141 organizations, including companies, international organizations, and foreign governments. These organizations are either located or have headquarters in 15 countries and represent 20 major sectors, from information technology to financial services. Of those organizations penetrated, 81 percent were either located in the United States or had US-based headquarters. According to Mandiant, Unit 61398, gained access to a wide variety of intellectual property and proprietary information through these intrusions.[62] Unit 61398 is the Second Bureau of the PLA's technical reconnaissance department, based in Shanghai.[63]

- In another high-profile example of a Chinese company allegedly targeting a US company's intellectual property through cyber espionage, the Department of Justice (DoJ) in June 2013 filed charges against Sinovel Wind Group, a Chinese energy firm, alleging Sinovel stole intellectual property from Massachusetts-based company American Superconductor (AMSC).[64] Once Sinovel was able to reproduce AMSC's technology after stealing its proprietary source code, the Chinese firm broke the partnership, cancelled existing orders, and devastated AMSC's revenue. AMSC has sought compensation from Sinovel through lawsuits in China, an effort which is ongoing and has resulted in legal fees for AMSC exceeding $6 million.[65] While these lawsuits continue to move slowly through the Chinese legal system, adding to AMSC's legal fees, Sinovel is reaping the profits of stolen technology.[66]

Deterring Chinese Cyber Theft

It is clear that attempting to name the perpetrators in China in an attempt to shame the Chinese government is not sufficient to deter Chinese entities from conducting cyber espionage against US companies. Mitigating the problem will require a well-coordinated approach across the US government and with industry. Many potential actions are being discussed by Congress, the Obama administration, and outside experts. These actions include linking economic cyber espionage to trade restrictions, prohibiting Chinese firms using stolen US intellectual property from accessing US banks, and banning US travel for Chinese organizations that are involved with cyber espionage. The US-China Economic and Security Review Commission recommends Congress take the following actions:

- Adopt legislation clarifying the actions companies are permitted to take regarding tracking intellectual property stolen through cyber intrusions.

- Amend the Economic Espionage Act (18 U.S.C. § 1831-1839) to permit a private right of action when trade secrets are stolen.

- Support the administration's efforts to achieve a high standard of protection of intellectual property rights in the Trans-Pacific Partnership and the Transatlantic Trade and Investment Partnership.

- Encourage the administration to partner with other countries to establish an international list of individuals, groups, and organizations engaged in commercial cyber espionage. The administration and partner governments should develop a process for the list's validation, adjudication, and shared access.

- Urge the administration to continue to enhance its sharing of information about cyber threats with the private sector, particularly small- and medium-sized companies.

My personal view is that the president already has the authority to place sanctions on Chinese persons, government industries, and companies through the International Emergency Economic Powers Act.[67] If the magnitude of the damage to the US economy is as great as that cited by General Alexander, the president should exercise that authority.

Sustaining the US Military's "Rebalance" to Asia

In January 2012, DoD's *Defense Strategic Guidance* declared the US military will "of necessity rebalance toward the Asia Pacific" by emphasizing existing alliances, expanding its networks of cooperation with "emerging" partners, and investing in military capabilities to ensure access to and freedom to maneuver within the region.[68] US Chief of Naval Operations ADM Jonathan Greenert explained the US Navy's role in the rebalance: "As directed by the 2012 *Defense Strategic Guidance* . . . the [US] Navy formulated and implemented a plan to rebalance our forces, their homeports, our capabilities, and our intellectual capital and partnerships toward the Asia Pacific."[69] Specifically, the US Navy aims to increase its presence in the Asia Pacific from about 50 ships in 2013 to 60 ships by 2020 and "rebalance homeports to 60 percent" in the region by 2020.[70]

However, the commission's annual report notes that US Defense Secretary Chuck Hagel in July 2013 said Washington would have to choose between a smaller, modern military and a larger, older one if sequester-level funding continues.[71] Admiral Greenert has warned constraints in the current budget environment could delay or prevent the US Navy from achieving its objectives in the rebalance.[72] There is growing concern in the United States and among US allies and partners that the DoD will be unable to follow through on its commitment to the rebalance due to declining defense budgets and emerging crises elsewhere in the world. This could lead some regional countries to increasingly accommodate China or pursue military capabilities that could be used offensively or preemptively. Either scenario could undermine US interests in the region.

I urge you to keep in mind that by 2020, China could have a navy and air force in Asia that outnumbers and almost matches the technical capability of our own forces. If our military force shrinks because of our own budget problems, we may have 60 percent of our forces in the Asia-Pacific region, but 60 percent of 200 ships is far less than 60 percent of a 300-ship navy. That may not be sufficient to deter China or to reassure our friends and allies in the region.

Larry M. Wortzel, PhD
US-China Economic and
Security Review Commission

Dr. Wortzel was appointed a member of the US-China Economic and Security Review Commission in 2001 and served two terms as its chair. He is a retired US Army colonel who spent much of his 32-year military career in the Asia-Pacific region. Colonel Wortzel was assistant Army attaché in China from 1988 to 1990 and Army attaché in China from 1995 to 1997. He is the author of *The Dragon Extends its Reach: Chinese Military Power Goes Global* (Potomac Books, 2013). A graduate of the Armed Forces Staff College and the US Army War College, Wortzel earned his MA and PhD in political science from the University of Hawaii.

Notes

1. The complete report can be found at http://www.uscc.gov/Annual_Reports/2013-annual-report-congress.

2. "Anti-access" (A2) actions are those intended to slow deployment of an adversary's forces into a theater or cause the forces to operate from distances farther from the conflict than they would otherwise prefer. A2 affects movement into theater. "Area denial" (AD) actions are those intended to impede an adversary's operations within areas where friendly forces cannot or will not prevent access. AD affects movement within theater. *Air Sea Battle: Service Collaboration to Address Anti-Access & Area Denial Challenges* (Arlington, VA: US Air-Sea Battle Office, May 2013), 2–4.

3. "Chinese Aircraft Carrier Returns to Home Port," *Renmin Ribao* (*People's Daily*), 22 September 2013, http://english.peopledaily.com.cn/90786/8407244.html; "China's Carrier-Borne Jet Pilots Receive Certification," Xinhua, 4 July 2013, http://english.peopledaily.com.cn/90786/8310416.html; "China's First Aircraft Carrier Leaves Homeport for Sea Trials," Xinhua, 11 June 2013, http://news.xinhuanet.com/english/china/2013-06/11/c_132447284.htm; "China's Aircraft Carrier Anchors in Military Port," Xinhua, 7 February 2013, http://www.china.org.cn/china/NPC_CPPCC_2013/2013-02/27/content_28071340.htm; and "China Now Capable to Deploy Jets on Aircraft Carrier: Navy," Xinhua, 25 November 2013, OSC ID: CPP20121125968098, http://www.opensource.gov.

4. *Annual Report to Congress: Military and Security Developments Involving the People's Republic of China 2013* (Washington: DoD, 2013), 31.

5. *The People's Liberation Army Navy: A Modern Navy with Chinese Characteristics* (Suitland, MD: Office of Naval Intelligence [ONI], 2009), 23.

6. *PLA Navy Orders of Battle 2000–2020,* written response to request for information provided to the US-China Economic and Security Review Commission (Suitland: ONI, 24 June 2013); and *Annual Report to Congress,* 10, 31.

7. *Annual Report to Congress,* 6–7; and J. Michael Cole, "China's Growing Long-Range Strike Capability," *Diplomat,* 13 August 2012, http://thediplomat.com/flashpoints-blog/2012/08/13/chinas-growing-long-range-strike-capability/.

8. Andrew Erickson and Gabe Collins, "China Carrier Demo Module Highlights Surging Navy," *National Interest,* 6 August 2013, http://nationalinterest.org/commentary/china-carrier-demo-module-highlights-surging-navy-8842; *PLA Navy Orders of Battle 2000–2020*; and *Annual Report to Congress,* 5–7.

9. *PLA Navy Orders of Battle 2000–2020.*

10. Ibid.

11. On tactical nuclear weapons including torpedoes, mines, antiship cruise missiles, and ADMs/mines, see Robert S. Norris, Andrew S. Burrows, and Richard W. Fieldhouse, *British, French, and Chinese Nuclear Weapons, Nuclear Weapons Databook,* vol. 5 (Boulder, CO: Westview Press, 1994), 359; Gregory B. Owens, "Chinese Tactical Nuclear Weapons" (master's thesis, Naval Postgraduate School, June 1996), 4; "Global Nuclear Stockpiles, 1945–1997," *Bulletin of the Atomic Scientists,* November/December 1997, 67; "Estimated Nuclear Stockpiles 1945–1993," *Bulletin of the Atomic Scientists,* December 1993, 57; and Robert S. Norris,

"Nuclear Arsenals of the United States, Russia, Great Britain, France and China: A Status Report," presentation at the 5th ISODARCO Beijing Seminar on Arms Control, Chengdu, China, November 1996. On torpedoes, see "Archive of Nuclear Data," http://www.nrdc.org /nuclear/nudb/datab17.asp; and Ronald O'Rourke, *China Naval Modernization* (Washington: Congressional Research Service [CRS], 5 September 2013), http://www.fas.org/sgp/crs /row/RL33153.pdf. According to sinodefense.com, in December 2005 China purchased Type-53-65 torpedoes from Russia and 40 Shkval torpedoes in 1998.

12. "China 'Buys Fighter Jets and Submarines from Russia,' " *BBC News*, 25 March 2013, http://www.bbc.co.uk/news/world-asia-21930280; and Robert Foster, "Russia to Sell, Co-Produce Lada-class Submarines to China," *Jane's Defence Weekly*, 20 December 2012, http:// www.janes.com/article/19682/russia-to-sell-co-produce-lada-class-submarines-to-china.

13. *PLA Navy Orders of Battle 2000–2020*; and *Annual Report to Congress*, 5–7.

14. Roger Cliff, "Chinese Military Aviation Capabilities, Doctrine, and Missions," in *Chinese Aerospace Power: Evolving Maritime Roles*, eds. Andrew S. Erickson and Lyle J. Goldstein (Annapolis, MD: Naval Institute Press, 2011), 252; and Richard Fisher, "Deterring China's Fighter Buildup," *Defense News*, 19 November 2012, http://www.defensenews.com /article/20121119/DEFFEAT05/311190005/.

15. *Annual Report to Congress*, 8; and Fisher, "Deterring China's Fighter Buildup."

16. "Summary: PRC Expert Says Yun-20 Transport Makes Strategic Air Force Possible," OSC ID: CPP20130128787028, Open Source Center, 27 January 2013, http://www.open source.gov.

17. "Summary: Guangdong Journal Views Strategic Card of 'Yun-20' Jumbo Air Freighter," OSC ID: CPP20130214695013, 31 January 2013; and Andrew Erikson and Gabe Collins, "The Y-20: China Aviation Milestone Means New Power Projection," *Wall Street Journal: China Real Time Blog*, 28 January 2013, http://blogs.wsj.com/chinarealtime/2013/01/28/the-y -20-china-aviation-milestone-means-new-power-projection/.

18. Zachary Keck, "Can China's New Strategic Bomber Reach Hawaii?" *Diplomat*, 13 August 2013, http://thediplomat.com/flashpoints-blog/2013/08/13/can-chinas-new-strategic-bomber -reach-hawaii/?utm_source=feedburner&utm_medium=feed&utm_campaign=Feed%3A+the -diplomat +%28The+Diplomat+RSS%29; Noam Eshel, "Chinese Air Force Gets More H-6K Strategic Bombers," *Defense Update*, 25 June 2013, http://defense-update.com/20130625_h-6k -bombers-delivered-to-pla-air-force.html; and Chen Boyuan, "H-6K Bombers Delivered to PLA Air Force," *China.org*, 22 June 2013, http://www.china.org.cn/china/2013-06/22 /content_29197824.htm.

19. *Annual Report to Congress*, 33, 42, 81.

20. Ian Easton, *The Assassin under the Radar: China's DH-10 Cruise Missile Program* (Arlington, VA: Project 2049 Institute, October 2009), 1–6, http://project2049.net/documents /assassin_under_radar_china_cruise_missile.pdf.

21. Keck, "Can China's New Strategic Bomber Reach Hawaii?"

22. Andrea Shalal-Esa, "RPT-China's Space Activities Raising U.S. Satellite Security Concerns," Reuters, 14 January 2013, http://www.reuters.com/article/2013/01/14/china-usa -satellites-idUSL2N0AJ10620130114; "Beijing to Trigger Arms Race by Testing Anti-Satellite Missiles," Central News Agency (Taipei), 13 January 2013, OSC ID: CPP20130115968204; Gregory Kulacki, "Is January Chinese ASAT Testing Month?" *All Things Nuclear, Insights on Science and Security*, 4 January 2013, http://allthingsnuclear.org/is-january-chinese-asat-testing -month/; *China: PLA Activities Report 16–31 Oct 2012* (Washington: DoD, 31 October 2012), OSC ID: CPP20121120440020; "China Dismisses Report on Planned Test Launch of Anti-Satellite Missile," Xinhua, 25 October 2012, OSC ID: CPP20121025968325; and Bill Gertz, "China to Shoot at High Frontier," *Washington Free Beacon*, 16 October 2012, http://freebeacon.com/china-to-shoot-at-high-frontier/.

23. Gregory Kulacki, " 'Kuaizhou' Challenges U.S. Perceptions of Chinese Military Space Strategy," *All Things Nuclear, Insights on Science and Security*, 27 September 2013, http://allthingsnuclear.org/kuaizhou-challenges-u-s-perceptions-of-chinese-military-space-strategy/.

24. *Annual Report to Congress*, 35–36.

25. "'Beidou,' China's Pride," *Bingqi Zhishi* (*Ordnance Knowledge*), 1 August 2012, OSC ID: CPP20121016680010.

26. "China Targeting Navigation System's Global Coverage by 2020," Xinhua, 3 March 2012, http://news.xinhuanet.com/english/sci/2013-03/03/c_132204892.htm.

27. "Navy North Sea Fleet's New Smart Target Ship Emits Electromagnetic Jamming against Missiles," *PLA Daily*, 4 August 2013, OSC ID: CHO2013080530196614; Yu Hu, "PLA Jinan MR Extends Military Use of the Beidou Satellite Navigation System," *Jinan Qianwei Bao* (*Jinan Front News*), 17 January 2012, OSC ID: CPP20130222667020; and Sun Chao, Zhang Jun, and Wang Jun, "PLA Chengdu MR Sichuan Div Uses Satellite Navigation to Standardize Time," *Chengdu Zhanqi Bao* (*Chengdu Battle Standard News*), 3 November 2011, OSC ID: CPP20130223667002.

28. Bill Gertz, "China Conducts another Mobile ICBM Test," *Washington Free Beacon*, 14 August 2013, http://freebeacon.com/china-conducts-another-mobile-icbm-test/.

29. *Annual Report to Congress*, 30; and Bill Gertz, "Riding the Nuclear Rails," *Washington Free Beacon*, 25 January 2013, http://freebeacon.com/riding-the-nuclear-rails/.

30. *Annual Report to Congress*, 36.

31. "Facts Figures: China's 2013 Draft Budget Report," Xinhua, 5 March 2013, OSC ID: CPP20130305968101; "China Boosts Defense Spending as Military Modernizes Arsenal," Bloomberg, 5 March 2013, http://www.bloomberg.com/news/2013-03-05/china-boosts -defense-spending-as-military-modernizes-its-arsenal.html; Luo Zheng, "Investment in Our National Defense Expenditure Mutually Conforms with National Security and Development Interests—Interview with Sun Huangtian, Deputy Director of PLA General Logistics Department, on 2013 National Defense Budget," *PLA Daily*, 6 March 2013, OSC ID: CPP20130307088001; "China Boosts Defense Spending as Military Modernizes Arsenal," Bloomberg, 5 March 2013, http://www.bloomberg.com/news/2013-03-05/china-boosts -defense-spending-as-military-modernizes-its-arsenal.html.

32. Adam Liff and Andrew Erickson, "Demystifying China's Defence Spending: Less Mysterious in the Aggregate," *China Quarterly*, 2013, http://journals.cambridge.org/action /displayAbstract?fromPage=online&aid=8874207.

33. Institute of International Strategic Studies, "China's Defence Spending: New Questions," *Strategic Comments*, 2 August 2013, http://www.iiss.org/en/publications/strategic%20 comments/sections/2013-a8b5/china--39-s-defence-spending--new-questions-e625.

34. *Annual Report to Congress*, 45.

35. Ibid., 69–71. These contacts include high-level visits, recurrent exchanges, academic exchanges, functional exchanges, and joint exercises.

36. Shirley Kan, *U.S.–China Military Contacts: Issues for Congress* (Washington: CRS, 25 July 2013).

37. Karen Parrish, "U.S.–China Military Ties Growing, Pacom Commander Says," US Armed Forces Press Service, 11 July 2013, http://www.defense.gov/news/newsarticle .aspx?id=120440.

38. Michelle Tan, "Army Hosts China in First Joint Field Exercise," *Army Times*, 12 November 2013, http://www.armytimes.com/article/20131112/NEWS/311120006/Army -hosts-China-first-joint-field-exercise.

39. Caitlin Campbell and Craig Murray, *China Seeks a "New Type of Major-Country Relationship" with the United States* (Washington: U.S.–China Economic and Security Review Commission, 25 June 2013), http://origin.www.uscc.gov/sites/default/files/Research /China%20Seeks%20New%20Type%20of%20Major-Country%20Relationship%20 with%20United%20States_Staff%20Research%20Backgrounder.pdf and Michael S. Chase,

"China's Search for a 'New Type of Great Power Relationship,'" *Jamestown Foundation China Brief* 12, no. 27 (7 September 2012): 14, http://www.jamestown.org/uploads/media/cb_09_04.pdf.

40. Larry M. Wortzel, *The Dragon Extends its Reach: Chinese Military Power Goes Global* (Washington: Potomac Books, 2013) 17, 40–41, 134, 145–48.

41. Dan Mcwhorter, "APT1 Three Months Later—Significantly Impacted, Though Active & Rebuilding," *M-unition*, 21 May 2013, https://www.mandiant.com/blog/apt1 -months-significantly-impacted-active-rebuilding/; and Richard Bejtlich (chief security officer at Mandiant), telephone interview with commission staff, 21 August 2013.

42. *Directory of PRC Military Personalities* (Washington: Defense Intelligence Agency, March 2013).

43. Ibid.

44. William C. Hannas, James Mulvenon, and Anna B. Puglisi, *Chinese Industrial Espionage: Technology Acquisition and Military Modernization*, (London and New York: Routledge, 2013), 226.

45. "2013 Nian 2 Yue 19 Ri Waijiaobu Fayanren Honglei Zhuchi Lixing Jizhehui (Ministry of Foreign Affairs Spokesperson Hong Lei Presides over Regular Press Conference 19 February 2013)," Ministry of Foreign Affairs, Beijing, http://www.fmprc.gov.cn/mfa_chn /fyrbt_602243/t1014798.shtml.

46. U.S.–China Economic and Security Review Commission, *2012 Annual Report to Congress* (Washington: Government Printing Office, November 2012), 166.

47. A honeypot is part of a honeynet, which is a fake or diversionary computer network designed to draw in an adversary to identify the adversary or give the adversary false information. Honeynets can provide intelligence regarding adversaries' "tools, tactics, and motives." Honeynet Project, "Short Video Explaining Honeypots," http://old.honeynet.org/misc/files /HoneynetWeb.mov.

48. Tom Simonite, "Chinese Hacking Team Caught Taking over Decoy Water Plant," *MIT Technology Review*, 2 August 2013, http://www.technologyreview.com/news/517786 /chinese-hacking-team-caught-taking-over-decoy-water-plant/.

49. Wortzel, *Dragon Extends its Reach*, 142.

50. Ellen Nakashima, "Confidential Report Lists U.S. Weapons System Designs Compromised by Chinese Cyberspies," *Washington Post*, 27 May 2013, http://www.washingtonpost .com/world/national-security/confidential-report-lists-us-weapons-system-designs-compromised -by-chinese-cyberspies/2013/05/27/a42c3e1c-c2dd-11e2-8c3b-0b5e9247e8ca_story.html.

51. Ibid.

52. National Defense Authorization Act for Fiscal Year 2011 (P. L. 111-383), 111th Cong., 2nd sess., 7 January 2011, http://www.gpo.gov/fdsys/pkg/PLAW-111publ383/pdf /PLAW-111publ383.pdf.

53. Special assistant to the DoD chief information officer, Office of the Assistant Secretary of Defense for Legislative Affairs, e-mail interview with commission staff, 28 May 2013.

54. Leigh Ann Ragland et al., *Red Cloud Rising: Cloud Computing in China* (Vienna, VA: Defense Group Inc. for the U.S.–China Economic and Security Review Commission, September 2013), 32–34, http://origin.www.uscc.gov/sites/default/files/Research/Red%20 Cloud%20Rising_Cloud%20Computing%20in%20China.pdf.

55. Ibid., 39.

56. Ibid., 38.

57. Josh Rogin, "NSA Chief: Cybercrime Constitutes the 'Greatest Transfer of Wealth in History,'" *Foreign Policy*, 9 July 2012, http://thecable.foreignpolicy.com/posts/2012/07/09 /nsa_chief_cybercrime_constitutes_the_greatest_transfer_of_wealth_in_history.

58. Mike McConnell, Michael Chertoff, and William Lynn, "China's Cyber Thievery is a National Policy—And Must Be Challenged," *Wall Street Journal*, 27 January 2012, http:// online.wsj.com/article/SB10001424052970203718504577178832338032176.html.

59. Commission on the Theft of Intellectual Property, *The IP Commission Report* (Washington: National Bureau of Asian Research, May 2013), 12, http://ipcommission.org/report /IP_Commission_Report_052213.pdf; and U.S.–China Economic and Security Review Commission, *2012 Annual Report to Congress*, 156.

60. In the late 1980s and early '90s a debate took place in Congress on whether the US intelligence community (IC) should share information and/or intelligence assets with US companies to provide those companies an advantage against foreign competitors. In 1991, Director of the Central Intelligence Agency Robert Gates, in a speech to the IC, stated clearly that the CIA would limit itself to helping US companies safeguard themselves from foreign intelligence operations. Robert Gates, "The Future of American Intelligence," speech to US intelligence community, Washington, DC, 4 December 1991.

61. Commission on the Theft of American Intellectual Property, *IP Commission Report*, 3, 18.

62. *APT1: Exposing One of China's Cyber Espionage Units* (Alexandria, VA: Mandiant, February 2013), 2, 3, 4, 9, 21–23, http://intelreport.mandiant.com/Mandiant_APT1_Report.pdf.

63. *APT1*, 9.

64. "Sinovel Corporation and Three Individuals Charged in Wisconsin with Theft of AMSC Trade Secrets," Department of Justice press release, 27 June 2013, http://www.justice .gov/opa/pr/2013/June/13-crm-730.html.

65. Melanie Hart, "Criminal Charges Mark New Phase in Bellwether U.S.–China Intellectual Property Dispute," Center for American Progress, Washington, DC, 27 June 2013, http://www.americanprogress.org/issues/china/news/2013/06/27/68339/criminal-charges -mark-new-phase-in-bellwether-u-s-china-intellectual-property-dispute/.

66. Ibid.

67. 50 U.S.C. § 1701, http://uscode.house.gov/view.xhtml?path=/prelim@title50 /chapter35&edition=prelim.

68. *Sustaining U.S. Global Leadership: Priorities for 21st Century Leadership* (Washington: DoD, January 2012), http://www.defense.gov/news/Defense_Strategic_Guidance.pdf.

69. Jonathan Greenert, "Foreword," in *U.S. Navy Program Guide 2013* (Washington: DoD, 2013), http://www.navy.mil/navydata/policy/seapower/npg13/top-npg13.pdf.

70. *U.S. Navy Program Guide 2013*.

71. "Statement on Strategic Choices and Management Review, Pentagon press briefing remarks by Secretary of Defense Chuck Hagel," Washington, DC, 31 July 2013, http://www .defense.gov/speeches/speech.aspx?speechid=1978.

72. House Committee on Armed Services, *Hearing on Planning for Sequestration in FY 2014 and Perspectives of the Military Services on the Strategic Choices and Management Review*, 113th Cong., 1st sess., 18 September 2013.

Disclaimer

The views and opinions expressed or implied in SSQ are those of the authors and are not officially sanctioned by any agency or department of the US government. We encourage you to send comments to: strategicstudiesquarterly@us.af.mil.

www.ingramcontent.com/pod-product-compliance
Lightning Source LLC
Chambersburg PA
CBHW080404290526
45790CB00009BA/3704